Trophy Mom

Trophy Mom

Hope Springs
Maternal

Tracy Curtis

Ashton Publishing

Charlotte, North Carolina

Copyright © 2016 by Tracy Curtis

Most content previously published, in slightly different form, in the
    Charlotte Observer, 2006 – 2015

Cover by Melissa Gamez

Jacket and Interior Design by Diana Wade

All rights reserved

ISBN: 978-0-9970588-1-9

For Mom

My mother is a poem

I'll never be able to write,

though everything I write

is a poem to my mother.

~ Sharon Doubiago

Contents

About This Book

Trophy Mom. I wish. The closest I'll ever come to being called a trophy mom is if I'm the mom lugging the box of trophies out to the field.

It's not like I'm not trying; I do aspire to be the perfect mom. I think all moms do. We're trying to have it all, be it all, do it all — and look good doing it. We know it's impossible, but we still keep trying. And there's a lot of humor in that!

Even during spring — the season reserved to celebrate moms with a specially designated Mother's Day — Mother Nature clearly reminds us that we have to keep it light. If she wanted us to take spring seriously, she wouldn't have given us pollen, spring break and little league sports. All that did was create a lot of housework, a ton of laundry, the dilemma of what to do with our kids for ten days and the need for spreadsheets to track sports practices, games and carpools.

But like our favorite mother, Erma Bombeck, used to say, "If you can laugh at it, you can live with it."

And so I give you *Trophy Mom* — a collection of my favorite columns about mothers and the mother of all seasons, spring — and all of the hilarity that comes with it.

Because if you're waiting for life to be perfect . . . you're going to be waiting a while!

The Pursuit of Perfection

Comedian Steven Wright once said, "When I was in school the teachers told me practice makes perfect; then they told me nobody's perfect, so I stopped practicing."

I feel like that today. Like I can't do anything right, so what's the point? There are so many places in my life I fall short — as a mom and a wife. And my ideas of perfection overwhelm me.

Because ideally my house would always be clean. My car would have the new-car smell. And my children wouldn't have peanut butter in their hair where the gum used to be.

I'd dress really cute every day, and not because I tried, but because I would just have that many cute clothes in my closet. My walk-in closet. My custom designed walk-in California Closet, with little drawers for socks and earrings.

I'd have our meals planned and prepped a week ahead of time — three nutritious meals a day for six days and one organic pizza night. And I'd sort everybody's clothing by color. And fold it really cool like the guys at Gap.

I'd have a desk that didn't have anything on it but my laptop. No wires, no science experiment brewing in my two-day-old coffee cup. Just a thin laptop on a crisp, white desk. In a white room. With a beautiful slipcovered chair, without any mustard on it. And smooth jazz just playing out of nowhere.

I'd give the most eloquent toasts, tell the funniest jokes and offer the most inspirational prayers. And I'd remember my girlfriends' birthdays. And the names of their children. And where I parked the car.

And I'd have a vending machine at the back door with matching shoes and socks for everybody in the family. It would also have AA batteries. And stamps. And a spare remote for the TV.

My picture frames would be either all silver or all gold, but not both. I'd have photo albums cataloged by year and bound in leather. We'd make it to church every Sunday. Or at least not be sweating, fighting or crying when we got there. And my kids would think cartoons are for losers.

I'd always underpromise and overdeliver and never undercook or overpack. Or overeat or underdress. Or over-commit. Or oversleep. And I'd never have that week where we're out of everything. My pantry would stay stocked, I'd have the kids' Motrin *before* they got a fever and my hair dyed *before* the roots showed.

I'd have Halle Berry's body, Martha Stewart's skills, Sheryl Crow's voice and Angelina Jolie's husband. And my children would say "Yes, ma'am" and "Can we help?"

I'd be completely organized, my day perfectly balanced between time with my husband, time with my kids and time for me to meet with *Architectural Digest* about photographing my house.

But that's all in a perfect world. And it's just too hard to make all that happen. Besides, Steven Wright also says, "If at first you don't succeed, destroy all evidence that you tried."

Maybe that's the way to go.

MOM FAILS

Stumbling is not falling.
~ Malcolm X

(But it is if you stumble off a cliff.)
~ Tracy Curtis

Too Much on Your Plate

So I'm at a red light behind a very nice Lexus SUV — the kind of shiny car that says all is right with the world. And yet, the license plate reads LORDYHLP.

I get it. Trust me, I could easily have that message on my plate — and a flag flying from the antenna that reads, *I'm Failing Every Day* — and a giant banner running down the side of my car that screams, *I Have No Idea What I'm Doing!*

But I'm not going to *out* myself like that. Yes, I'm trying to be perfect and it's not working. But I'm not going to advertise it to the masses. I'm on the fake-it-till-you-make-it program. I give the *appearance* I've got it under control. It's the next best thing to the truth, and maybe over time I'll actually get there.

So if I were going to personalize my plate, I'd go with MOMROX. No, I'm not rocking anything at the moment, but nobody has to know that. And this way, I stay positive, optimistic and in a reasonable amount of denial, all while building confidence with my false sense of achievement.

The fact that I overslept and am late getting kids to school doesn't need to make the PTA newsletter. So I no longer race over there in pajamas; I throw on workout clothes. It gives the impression I squeezed in a run before carpool, or at the very least, was busy getting ready for that cardio class I'm headed to. And who knows, maybe one day I'll go.

Same with the grocery. I don't advertise that it's been two weeks by creating a giant landfill of food in my large cart. I pick one day to go, but then I go several times — using one of those little baskets. So it looks like I'm thoroughly stocked at home, but just running in to get a few things for dinner. Pick up a seafood seasoning and people think you're pan-searing fish. Seriously.

Change your hair, earrings and your scarf color each day, and I promise you nobody at the office will realize you're wearing the same black pants and white shirt. How infrequently you do your laundry is not for public consumption.

And when folks drop by on short notice and the kitchen's a wreck, pull out all your cookware, put it on the stove, turn on the burners and use the empty cabinet to hide the dirty dishes, newspapers, dog bowl and shoes. It'll appear totally clean. And that you're preparing a four-course dinner.

The point is, nobody needs to know you need help — they just need to know you don't appear to need any. The only time a mom should hang LORDYHLP on the back of her car is if she's gotten trapped in the trunk.

But maybe she wasn't driving her car. Maybe it was her husband's car. In which case, that license plate probably works.

With a Cherry on Top

So when I wrote that column about the LORDYHLP license plate, I didn't consider the possibility that the driver of the car would run me down. But she did, and here's what happened . . .

Her name is Linda Cherry — married nearly forty years and mother to four boys and one girl — Tripp, Trent, Trigg, Trevor and Traci, ages 30-37. After reading the article, her son Trigg emailed me, wanting me to know some things about his mother and her LORDYHLP tag . . .

She's as put together of a woman as you'll ever find. She always had her stuff together. Her "Lordy helps" were reserved for when, on rare moments, she was at the very edge of flipping out on one of us (and I'm sure when that time came, we COMPLETELY deserved it). It didn't happen often and the other 99% of the time she was the lady most women are faking to be like. She always kept a clean house, a fridge full of groceries, clothes washed, and made every one of us feel loved, important, smart and needed.

It was such a beautiful letter, and I really wanted to know how to raise children who don't grow up to think their mom's a crazy person. Her son set us up for coffee — and walking into IHOP it was easy to spot this attractive, petite woman with beautiful white hair, impeccably dressed for her bridge game.

I gave her every opportunity to cop to the struggle, fear, insecurity and anxiety we have as mothers. And while she acknowledged there seems to be more pressure for my generation of moms, it was always just real simple to her. She loved babies and she loved having children. She sent her kids outside to play. Told them to run with good kids. Talked about drugs and alcohol and spent a lot of time together as a family. In fact, she said the most important thing you can give a child is time.

And she wasn't talking about time planning birthday parties, registering for camp, driving to multiple sports practices and emailing about play dates. And certainly not time worrying if I'm doing it right. Or trying to make it look like I am.

Because maybe I'm not doing it as well as somebody else, or as easily as the next mom. But the good news is there's absolutely no pressure in making a child feel "loved, important, smart and needed." In fact, if that's all I did, I would actually feel like I was doing a great job.

So thank you, Linda, for sharing your wisdom, your spirit and your license plate. Just one more question . . .

How do you get your kids to write letters?

This Doesn't Add Up

My little boy plops down at the kitchen counter and asks if I can help with his math. His first problem is:

Each of three girls is on exactly one team. One is on the field hockey team, another is on the swimming team and the third is on the track team. Ann is not on the swimming team. The girl on the track team lives near Ann. The girl on the swimming team and Betty are in the same class. What team is Carol on?

Are you kidding me? I guess math isn't math anymore. Apparently it's English. The math I took in elementary school had actual numbers in it. This isn't even English, this is *gossip* — no doubt being passed around by a bunch of moms who have nothing better to do.

What team is Carol on? It's none of my business! I'm sure

she's on the team of the sport she loves to play and she's doing her thing. I *have* a life; I don't need to be all up in Carol's.

Each of the three girls is on exactly one team. I'm sure they are. I'm sure their moms are friends and they all got together and agreed that each child should do one sport to better focus on school, friends and family and not be torn between their many fabulous talents. Which translates into three moms who don't want to drive all over town all week.

Ann is not on the swimming team. What's up with that? Sounds like there's a story there. She didn't make it? Or did her mom forget to register online? I don't know, but it seems like it was definitely worth mentioning, so I don't imagine we'll be seeing Ann swimming anytime soon.

The girl on the track team lives near Ann. So why aren't they carpooling? Those two should be doing the same sport. Well, unless it's the swimming, of course — I'm thinking Ann is afraid of the water or something. Regardless, neighbors need to all do the same thing. Trust me; we've got seven city blocks playing Charlotte United soccer over here.

The girl on the swimming team and Betty are in the same class. Oh, okay, so they're probably besties because everybody knows your best friends are your classmates and not the most convenient choice of the child who lives nearby.

I feel sorry for Ann. She doesn't have a friend in her class and she can't swim. Kids are so mean and people just need to mind their own business. All this speculation about who's doing what and where and with whom is not good for anyone.

And so I tell my son this one is bigger than us. And that this a problem that we are just not going to be able to solve.

He looks at me wide-eyed, slowly sliding his books off the counter.

"I think I'll just ask Dad."

To Coin a Phrase

My fifth grader grins. And motions for me to follow him to the den, where my second grader stands angry, in front of the TV. They are arguing over which channel to watch.

"Okay," he says to his little brother. "We'll toss a coin. Heads I win, tails you lose."

Ah, yes. The ole heads-I-win-tails-you-lose trick. I'm amused. And impressed. His delivery of the line is flawless — no smirk, or hint of a trick. He excitedly tosses the coin up, then eagerly looks to see what it is. Then gives a sort of *aw, too bad* look, as he delivers the bad news.

"Heads, I win."

My little guy explodes.

"Not AGAIN!"

Uh-oh. This isn't a new game. As a mother, who hates to see her baby being taken advantage of, I think it's mean. But as a woman who can't get this seven-year-old to just go with the flow, I think it's brilliant.

Instead of him pitching a fit and getting his way, we can now settle matters with a fair coin toss. Okay, not exactly fair. Except for the fact that he's being given a chance to catch on to this thing every time the coin goes into the air.

But he's not catching on. And he's getting mad. Internally, his chain is being jerked and he can't figure out why, and it's getting to him. He hasn't gotten the first turn, the last cookie or his TV pick in a week. He's wearing thin, and it's time to come clean.

We'll do it Sunday, before church. We'll confess, go pray and get brunch. Big brother strongly agrees — enough is enough, and we call him to the door.

But my youngest comes out, shoes in hand, and announces that he is *not* going to church.

"Well, why don't we flip a coin?" I blurt out.

Oops. But, come on, I don't have time for his defiance. If we're late to church, they'll run out of coffee.

I elbow Mr. Vegas in the ribs. *Toss it.*

"Heads I win, tails you lose," he sheepishly mumbles.

Don't go soft on me now, Vegas; they'll run out of donuts, too. He weakly tosses up the coin and can barely look at it.

"Tails, you lose."

My baby glares at the coin. Then back up at us, his eyeballs actually quivering in their sockets. His face turns real red. I think he's put it together. We take a giant step back . . .

"Well? LET'S GO!"

And he storms out the front door. And we make it to church on time. Which, can I just point out, is what *should* be happening, without us having to flick coins all around.

So, do we tell him and continue to battle it out all spring? Or stay mum and keep getting our way until summer starts?

It's a toss-up.

Hard Shoes to Fill

In line for shoes at a bowling alley, a woman next to us is saying someone stole her shoes. My friend grabs my arm and says she would be so mad if someone took her shoes — her leather boots from New York that fit her perfect.

I'd be mad too. I'm wearing my favorite leather riding boots, and I'm not about to just let them gallop out the door with some stranger. And why would anyone do that? Doesn't the phrase "walk a mile in my shoes" scare everybody?

Just this week I've been to Firestone, Autobell, Costco, the dentist and the vet. Walk a mile in my shoes and you're gonna need to sell them for money.

The manager hands me my pair and I'm reminded why nobody steals bowling shoes. This pair isn't the cute, narrow style — they're sort of a saddle shoe gone Bozo, with the extra-wide toe. They're like two-toned clown shoes.

This prompts my girlfriend to quickly hide our personal

shoes. She wraps our footwear in her coat, hides it under our table, then puts her bag atop the heap, making this the first time I've ever seen anyone hide their shoes under their purse.

After game one, my youngest treats dinner like a pizza-eating contest, and let's just say it ends with the two of us in a bathroom stall, with me compassionately muttering something along the lines of "Oh, sweetie, I told ya so."

I grab him and my coat, and we leave, and only when we get home do I realize . . . we're still wearing our bowling shoes.

How is this possible? Not only have I left my leather boots behind, but I've managed to steal a pair of shoes sure to get me recruited by Ringling Brothers. And bowling shoes are like pointe shoes and ski boots — you can only wear them to do *one* thing.

The next morning, I need to go out and get the paper and they're the only shoes near the door. What will the neighbors think? It'll be sort of a remix of the walk of shame, when you've stolen the shoes you're walking in.

Or maybe it's the walk of lame — where it appears you're just getting in from somewhere, but where you've been isn't that cool. I can hear the guy across the street . . .

"Big night of bowling, huh?"

I'll get the paper later. The last thing I need is for the bowling alley to refuse to take the shoes back because the bottoms are scuffed and I actually have to *buy* them. And then I look like some crazy mom, who lets her kid eat until he's sick, abandons expensive boots, then steals shoes that could only be worn if we join a mother-son bowling league or the circus.

Yeah, yeah, if the shoe fits . . .

Bat Out of Hell

Every now and then a mom finds herself alone in her house for the night. It's a little thrill, drifting off to sleep, knowing that no one's going to be waking me tonight.

Until midnight. Screeching shatters the silence, and I bolt out of bed to my door.

I peer into the hallway. Whatever it is, it's clearly in the house. It sounds like bats — trapped — trying to kill each other. I slam my bedroom door and start to call 911. The front door's locked, so they'll have to kick it in. But because I already know I am never going to sleep here again, I don't care.

Before I can dial I find myself making a run for it — the fear of something flying at my head and attacking my face is terrifying, but I have got to get out, and I literally fly over the staircase — I mean, I touch *maybe* five steps.

Now on the street in my pajamas with my cell phone, I'm

not sure what to do. I really want to call the police or animal control, but I don't have on enough clothes to stand around chitchatting about whatever is being torn to shreds inside my house.

I run up the street and breathlessly call and wake a neighbor.

"There's at least two of them, probably more!" I shriek, crying and shaking outside her front door. "Wild bats or something rabid, trapped in my son's bedroom!"

Minutes later her husband emerges dressed in jeans, boots and a hat, carrying a bucket, a broom, a collapsible cage, garbage bags and a hammer. His wife scuttles behind him in a furry blue bathrobe and flip-flops. And off we trek down the street.

Back in the house, we can still hear them. Whatever they are, they are *mad*. My neighbor, the bravest soul on this earth as far as I'm concerned, slowly ascends the stairs, followed by blue-bathrobe lady and me, clutching her arm, pulling clumps of fur out of her robe.

It's definitely coming from the bedroom. And with the broom handle, he slowly pushes open the door. Then carefully peers into the dark room . . . leans in a little farther . . . and whispers:

"Is that . . . is that . . . a sound machine?"

He pushes through, walks up to the gadget, and hits Off. I collapse on the floor. I totally forgot I bought my son a sound machine last week. Somehow it got set to go off at twelve a.m. — and not to Wind Chimes, or Ebb Tide or Rain Shower. But Aviary. Which sounds an awful lot like, oh, I don't know — *Bats in a cage trying to kill each other!*

I feel bad. I look at my stunned neighbor, who looks like he's about to be deployed to Iraq. And his poor tired wife. And the clock, which changes to one a.m.

"Thanks for coming down and turning off my sound machine . . ."

I think we're still friends. Easier to make up with them than with the police after they've broken down my front door. Or an animal control unit after they've shot my sound machine with a tranquilizer gun.

And as for those sound machines?

They're for the birds.

Truth or Dare

I'm teaching character education at the elementary school, and the monthly trait is honesty. So I kick it off with my story of when I was six and stole a pack of Juicy Fruit from a Walmart.

Kids love that story. I took the gum, got it all the way home, then pretended to "find it" in the car. Then my Dad dragged me back to the Walmart, where I had to go into the store, tell the manager I stole from him, return the gum and apologize — all while bawling my eyes out.

I never forgot it; it was traumatic, impactful, and I never stole anything ever again.

The kids are absolutely wide-eyed. They appear traumatized too. One little boy says he can't take listening to the story, while another says how scary it is. Good. I'm changing the name of this thing. I'm calling it "Character Ed: Scared Straight."

But . . . there's always one. A kid wants to know why I didn't just hide the gum until I got in the house, then nobody would know I even had it.

"*I* would know," I say slowly, ominously — a little annoyed that he sliced through the awesome dramatic tension I'd unintentionally created. To which he just shrugs and goes back to doodling — no doubt a pack of gum with *Free* written above it.

Then we role-play: a girl walks past a ten-dollar bill lying on the ground outside her classroom — what should she do? She says give it to an adult so they can find the owner. But again, Mr. Juicy Fruit raises his hand and says he'd just keep it. Who would know?

Again — *you* would know. More doodling — my guess, a ten-dollar bill and *Just Do It*.

In the next scenario, a student is trying to get her friend to give her an answer on a test. She says, no, it's cheating. But ole Juicy Fruit has a better idea. Why not give her the wrong answer so she'll miss it. Great idea. Teach your friend a lesson about cheating — by lying.

Character assassination is one thing, but this is character suicide. I'm actually wondering how many library books this kid's got past due. I quickly wrap things up, grab my honesty literature and start for the door. But he follows me and asks what if he's a twin, and his twin commits a crime, but they blame . . .

I run into the hall and scour the character trait list to see what's next. Justice.

Oh boy, are we gonna have fun role-playing that.

THE MOTHER OF ALL SEASONS

Mother Nature changes her looks for the same reason any
woman changes her looks — to be noticed.
~ Richelle E. Goodrich

Don't Mess with Mother Nature

There is no doubt that the mother of all mothers is in charge of spring. Just the fact that the season is called *spring* says it all: everybody up, don't walk — *leap* — because it is *on*.

And so is Mother Nature. First thing she does is spring us ahead a whole hour into time. So awesome. We're gonna eat breakfast in the dark, so we can maximize our daylight hours. And because she puts a spring in our step, we become more active and productive than we've been all winter.

We get out, we cut grass, we wash cars. We plant flowers, grow vegetables and run 5Ks. We make slaw and buy hammocks. We paint the houses and meet the neighbors. We pick strawberries, make shortcakes and improve our short game.

Because she makes outside so magical. It's like Dorothy landing in Munchkinland. Overnight, the flowers bloom. The grass turns green, the air blows warm and we get squirrels, Easter bunnies and leprechauns — and an entire day dedicated to hiding colorful eggs full of chocolate gold coins!

And oh, the shopping, she's totally got that covered. All the clothes are lighter and brighter — you can wear pink, paisley and polka dots. And that's just the jacket. Anything goes — purple, orange, yellows and greens. Strappy sandals and sparkly tees. Mix, match and make lemonade. Enjoy the spring sales.

And celebrate the fact that video is practically dead, because she has loaded up spring with outdoor sports. Kids play lacrosse, baseball and soccer, and it's not even virtual. And live music isn't what you watch on YouTube, it's outside in the park. In fact, the only app you need during spring is Google Maps, so you can find the field, zoo and outdoor amphitheater.

And we love spring cleaning, dedicated to all the stuff nobody wanted to deal with for nine months. Some things you clean, some things you burn. Either way, the windows are thrown wide open.

At some point you come down with a spring fever — where you can't even be inside. You cook outside. You eat outside, you drink outside. Your kids talk you into sleeping outside. But you don't have to; Lady Spring gave us an out — she gave us pollen.

She also gave us the Spring Fling. I think this varies from

person to person, but for me it's usually an outdoor party where I get to wear a floral dress. Spring break definitely varies from person to person. Spring break for me now is a well thought-out trip — whereas in college, it was definitely a trip, but without any thought whatsoever.

Lady Spring.

You go, girl!

Time Is on Your Side

Okay, so did we all survive daylight saving time? I can't believe it takes a whole week to recover from losing one crummy hour. I actually forgot about it. The microwave says it's 7:30. Minutes later the cable box says 8:40. Now that's freaky. I lost an hour just walking from the kitchen to the den.

What's even freakier is that the cable company is all of a sudden time sensitive. The people who can't nail down anything tighter than a four-hour window are now dictating precise, universal time. Why do they get to decide what time it is *and* what you get to watch on TV? We're all so worried about who's going to run the country; I think we should be worried about who's running the cable company.

They say the purpose of daylight saving is to make better use of daylight. Well if the cable company wants me to make better use of my time, they should give me more of it, not less.

And aren't the days long enough? I mean, is an extra hour of yelling for my kids to come inside really going to change anybody's life? Plus my youngest keeps arguing that it's lunchtime, not dinnertime, because it's light outside. He's trying to take us all the way back to noon, which would really make for a long day.

And you can take the hour out of the day, but you can't beat the ever-lovin' daylights out of your husband and his determination to stay on "real time." I can't feed anybody without him saying, "You're feeding him now? I know it says it's seven, but it's really six *his* time."

His time. What, does he live in Texas? I can't live in eastern time with two kids living in central. Every time I called them for dinner, I'd have to think about what time it is "out there."

People just can't let go. They live in the past hour because they cannot accept that the hour is really gone. And I know why this is. Because they didn't make use of the extra hour they were given back in October. They took that hour and they used it to sleep. They blew it — and they know it — and they can't deal with it.

That's why I always use that hour. Like two years ago, I used that time to stockpile in case of an ice storm. So when I lost an hour, I got to go into the garage and look at all my canned goods and bottled water. See? A tangible reminder that I used my time wisely.

Now if I were really smart, I would have scheduled my

inducement during that extra hour. Then when everybody's complaining that they completely lost an hour, I could say, *Not me, I had a baby!* I'd have that hour back, and also a constant reminder for the rest of my life that not even the cable company can take it away from me.

The point is, that hour doesn't have to be lost, any more than those four hours waiting on the cable guy. Just like you plan things to do while you're waiting on him, plan what you're going to do with that hour coming to you in the fall.

You'll sleep great. And you won't even have to use the extra hour to do it.

Nothing to Sneeze At

Spring has sprung and the pollen has popped. Bringing with it the itchy eyes, drippy nose and the funny sound it makes when you try to scratch your throat with your tongue. So here are a few refreshing ideas from everydayhealth.com to help you beat those allergies . . .

Wear Sunglasses to Keep Pollen Out of Your Eyes. Apparently wearing sunglasses outside can reduce the amount of pollen or spores that get into your eyes. They can also hide your red itchy eyes that your significant other is convinced is a bad case of pink eye.

Ditch Pollen-Producing Indoor Plants. It says indoor plant soil lets mold spores into your house, the biggest offenders being indoor shrubs, trees and grasses that may produce pollens. Can I just say as a big allergy sufferer, I would never have grass, shrubs or trees in my house. Not because of allergies, but because I don't want to have to mow or rake the living room.

Kill Dust Mites with a Hot Wash. It says microscopic insects called dust mites love to live on your bedding. Great. I think I'll reconsider that grass. I'd much rather ditch the bedroom and the insect-infested bed in favor of a campout in the living room in a sleeping bag.

Take a Vacation from Pollen. If you can identify your trigger season, you may be able to avoid the worst pollen exposure by getting out of town for part of it. It suggests the beach as a great place to escape from pollen. Perfect. Allergy vacations tend to be a bit longer than a holiday or spring break, but maybe your boss would approve you taking a season off.

Clean Trouble Spots for Indoor Allergy Control. This refers to windows, curtains, blinds, poorly ventilated laundry rooms, basements, refrigerator drain pans and old books. But I've done all this. I even got rid of the carpet, the rugs, the fine fabrics and fancy bedding. The poor cat can't even find a soft place to sleep! Oh wait . . . the cat . . .

Keep Outdoor Pollens Outside. Take some simple precautions to keep outdoor pollens out of your home. They suggest removing your yard work clothes before entering the house. I would just say, make sure the neighbors aren't home or you won't be the only one rubbing your eyes.

When you do laundry, use a dryer instead of hanging your clothes outside. I like this suggestion. If it's after 1938, go ahead and use the automatic dryer.

Get Rid of Roaches and Rats. Another good tip. In fact, this one's so good that even if I didn't have allergies I'd probably attack this one.

There are lots of things you can do to protect yourself from allergies. Personally I like popping a Zyrtec, wrapping myself in plastic wrap and then going about my day. It's not fashionable, but I'm safe from pollen.

And I can sweat off five pounds.

Today Will Be the Last

So I'm looking at my calendar, and on April the eleventh, I have penciled in *Last Day*. I noticed it last week, but I was thinking that it was the last day of Lent. But that's next Thursday. And then I thought maybe it's the last day to finish my taxes. But that's next week too.

So what in the world is this? I never write down something that's nothing. So this day is definitely the last day of . . . what? It's not the last day of spring. It's not the last day of pollen season. It's not even close to being the last day I sneeze this month, so I can't imagine why I wrote this.

Was I thinking that by this date I shouldn't be wearing something any longer? Like, last day to wear wool? Last day to wear boots? Last day to wear a coat, unless it's cotton in a spring pastel?

Or is it something I shouldn't be doing any longer? Like, last day to work out inside? Eat lunch indoors? Build a fire?

Run the heat? Run my mouth?

Maybe it has nothing to do with weather, but is some sort of drop-dead deadline I set for myself. Last day to throw out the Halloween candy. To switch out all the Christmas cocktail napkins that say *Eat, drink and who's Mary?* To put away the long johns and break out the Spanx.

Maybe it's the last day *before* something. The last day before I get fired. Or my house gets broken into. Or my kids run away from home. But how would I know that in advance? And why waste time noting it on my calendar instead of just doing a better job, setting the burglar alarm, and locking the kids in their rooms?

Maybe it was a secret message from my subconscious about something I inherently know I should have done by now. Last day to become gluten-free. Sugar-free. Carefree. Last day to write the great American novel. Or the mediocre Scottish handbook.

I can't figure it out. I'm going to go with the cocktail napkin thing. *Eat, drink and who's Mary?* gets replaced by *If you love southern women, raise your glass. If not, raise your standards.* Works year-round, and won't need to be rotated.

Walking my kids to the bus stop Friday, I decide maybe the Last Day is just that. The last day — on the planet. So be it; I won't have to go to the grocery store.

But then suddenly my son says, "I'm so glad it's the last day."

I whirl around.

"The last day of what, and why is it the last?"

"Mom, it's the last day before spring break."

Geesh. The napkin thing was better.

Spring Break Feels Broken

You know what I noticed last week? While we were on spring break, I realized that I say the *exact* same things on vacation that I do at home. I thought vacation was about ditching routine and mixing it up. But even over the break, mom's still a broken record.

At home it goes like this . . .

I walk into the kitchen, start the coffee and yell, "Who left out the milk?!" Then I call for everyone to get their shoes, grab their book bags and head for the bus — at which time I look around and then yell out into the street, "You better bring back my iPad!"

Then they're back from school. And I'm like, "Who's going to practice, do you need me to drive you, and don't forget to put on your sunscreen. Grab your lacrosse stick, you're about to forget your helmet — and go get my wallet, you might need some money."

And then it's dinnertime. The kids want food and ask what's for dinner. I give them three options, and they say, "That's it?" And I answer, "Well, there's always chicken fingers."

And at bedtime, it's "Brush your teeth, take a shower, and don't forget to hang up your towel. Repack your book bag, give me back my charger, and don't change the channel! I wanna watch *Nashville*."

And at the beach it goes like this . . .

I walk into the kitchen, start the coffee and yell, "Who left out the milk?!" Then I call for everyone to get their flip-flops, grab their towels and head for the beach — at which time I look around and then yell out into sand dunes, "You better bring back my iPad!"

Then they're back from the beach. And I'm like, "Who's going fishing, do you need my bike, and don't forget to put on your sunscreen. Grab your pole, you're about to forget your tackle box — and go get my wallet, you might need some money."

And then it's dinnertime. The kids want seafood and ask what's for dinner. The waitress gives them three specials, and they say, "That's it?" And she answers, "Well, there's always chicken fingers."

And at bedtime, it's "Brush off the sand, take a shower, and don't forget to hang up your bathing suit. Repack your beach bag, give me back my sunglasses, and don't change the channel! I wanna watch *Nashville*."

And this probably works anywhere. I could be in China and would still be saying the same thing over and over. I'm like the CD that gets stuck in the player, so it's the only thing that plays. I gotta switch things up. Next time we go to the beach, I'm making a *serious* change.

I'm not buying milk.

THE MOTHERLOAD

Housework, if you do it right, will kill you.
~ Erma Bombeck

Playing Dirty

Here they come. Barreling through the front door, fresh off the school bus. One backpack gets flung at a living room chair. The other gets slung to the sofa. Shoes drop like breadcrumbs from the front hall to the back den, where bags of chips are ripped open, crumbs falling to the floor. And you know what? I don't care. I used to care, but I don't anymore. Do you want to know why? Three little words: the Dirty Thirty.

The Dirty Thirty is something I created to restore some order around here. With the change in the weather, so came a change in the way we clean. It's a thirty-minute block of time allocated to the picking up, cleaning up and sweeping up of everything that's been scattered and strewn and basically slob-lobbed all over my nice house.

Here's how it goes: Each day I choose a time to cheerfully announce that it's time for the Dirty Thirty. At that point the electronics dim, the mouths close, the attitudes change and we begin a fast and furious overhaul of our dwelling. Doesn't matter if it's not your mess, or it's not your room. Because it's *our* house, therefore *our* mess, thus a group effort — as we load the dishwasher, take out the trash, unload the dryer and find all the remotes. We go room to room and do not move on until all is as it should be. We hang up clothes, we put away dishes, refresh the cat box and pull chips from the sofa.

Now here's the cool thing — since we do this every day, we can actually get our house together in about fifteen minutes. So does the Dirty Thirty become the Fevered Fifteen? Absolutely not, because there's always something to do, and this is brilliance of the thirty-minute rule.

This is where we go above and beyond. I get the kids to hang fresh towels, match all the socks and stand up all the boots in my closet. Color-code my sweaters, label the pantry shelves, sort the utensil drawer and figure out where that funny smell is coming from. They do what I tell them to do for thirty minutes. They prepped a taco bar — like I really want to shred lettuce and grate cheese. I had them do it. I didn't get my necklaces untangled, but there's always tomorrow.

It's awesome. It's understood, uninterrupted and universally accepted, now that I'm allowing music. In fact, tomorrow after they untangle my jewelry, I think I'll to get them to organize my playlists and get my pictures on that cloud. Maybe download some cooking apps — they'll think it's great. They'll practically be gaming and might actually get a decent meal out of it.

And then I tape two five-dollar bills to the fridge and tell them at the end of the week it's theirs. Everybody's happy. They earn a regular allowance and I have a clean house and get to wear necklaces again.

And all the socks match.

Can't Hack It

I am really getting into the life hacks. If you're not familiar with life hacking, it refers to any trick, shortcut, skill or novelty method that increases productivity and efficiency. I used to think that was just getting eight hours of sleep, but apparently there are many more tricks of the housekeeping trade.

For instance, use frozen grapes to chill your wine. And beeswax to waterproof your shoes. Put a wooden spoon across a boiling pot of water to keep it from boiling over, and use Doritos for kindling to start a fire. (For an outdoor bonfire, use the Fiery Habanero flavor, I'm guessing.)

If you don't have a corkscrew, hammer a nail into the cork and then use the nail remover on your hammer to pull it out. Or if you're in a hurry, just hit the bottle with the hammer. Then pair it with the walnuts you rubbed on your damaged wooden furniture to cover up the dings. You've solved two problems and kick-started happy hour.

Turn on your seat warmer on the passenger side to keep pizza hot while driving home. And I would think with the newer cars, you could probably fry an egg over there. Or at the very least, heat up your coffee during carpool.

Take pictures of friends holding items you've lent them with your iPhone, so you'll remember it down the road. Or my idea is to take pictures of friends holding something they own that you'd really like to have, and then later convince them that it belonged to you.

They say you can clean out an old lotion bottle and put your phone, money and keys in it for safer keeping at the beach. I was thinking this is risky, as lotion gets left in the sand or passed around the pool. But I suppose if that happened, you could just call it.

Use half a pool noodle taped to the wall to protect your car door from slamming against the garage wall. I thought that's what the kids' bikes were for, but whatever. And if you have an ant problem, spread cinnamon across the paths of where they're entering the rooms; they'll avoid it like the plague. Then all you'll have is a cinnamon problem.

To upgrade your doors to a furniture-like status, upholster a door in fabric and trim. Unless you have a cat. Or you don't want your living room to look like the inside of Jeannie's bottle. And if you accidentally close a tab, Ctrl+Shift+T reopens it. But this doesn't work on a Coke.

This last one says if you're having trouble sleeping, try blinking your eyes really fast for a minute, because tired eyes help you fall asleep quicker. This one's totally lame, because I'm sitting here blinking my eyes really, really fast and nothing's hap . . .

Scent of a Woman

I love it when the department stores send out direct mailers advertising their sales. And it's not the flyers about the shoes or the jackets or the cute skirts that I like. It's the perfume samples.

At first, I just liked to smell them. Then watch the kids fight over who gets to smell them first. But then one day, I forgot to put on my perfume and saw a sample sitting on the hall table. And so I just peeled back the flap and wiped the sheet of paper all over my shirt.

You wouldn't think it, but you can actually get about three days' worth of rubs out of those. After the second day, the adhesive under the flap wears down and you can rub it right onto your neck.

Seeing how powerful the scent is, I got the idea to open one up and leave it in my car. I can't tell you what an improvement it is over the fragrances you have to choose from at the car wash. I'll take Calvin Klein's Euphoria over New Car Smell any day.

It also beats air freshener. I always leave an opened sample on the table at the front door. Who doesn't want to be greeted every day by Marc Jacobs? Vera Wang's Lovestruck is perfect in my bathroom. And David Yurman is all over the bedroom.

My new thing is giving the furniture a little zip. This is where some of the male fragrances come in, because I get those, too. And there is nothing like a fine cologne for men. Especially when combined with a leather armchair. Just a quick little rub on the seat, and you're practically sitting in Ralph Lauren's lap.

I've got Ralph in the living room, Gucci in the office and Armani on all the dining chairs. And if you've been to my house and you've been trying to figure it out, that's Burberry on the hand towels in the guest bath.

I keep my girl Donna Karan in my purse. Makes opening it and taking out my wallet almost a pleasure. And in the mudroom to cover all the shoes, socks and jerseys, I stash Dolce & Gabbana. Because in there, it really does take two.

The only problem is it smells like a department store. I feel like I'm living in Macy's. The kids are sneezing, we can't taste our food, and sometimes when the men's colognes overlap, I get really insecure.

Good thing the smells wear off in a week.

Put It to Rest

So I'm at the gym and my friend tells me she doesn't have hot water. And I'm offering to have her come to my house to get her shower. But the whole time all I'm thinking is *I have to go make my bed.*

What's up with that? Why do we feel compelled to make our bed for the benefit of someone else? I didn't make it before. But because somebody's going to see it, now I want to do it. And why? So she'll see my nicely made bed and think, *Here's a gal who's so together she actually cleaned her room and made her bed, all before a workout, without even the first drop of coffee.*

It seems that would be the reason. But she's a close friend, so she's been in my car and in my kitchen. And every time she comes over the same magazine is still in the plastic. On top of the unopened mail. She already knows I'm not together. The only thing this bed-making thing is going to do is confuse her. Or make her wonder if I've turned my home into a bed and breakfast and if she's standing in one of the rooms that I rent.

But she won't wonder long. Because every time someone tells me how impressed they are that I made my bed, I immediately confess that the only reason I did it was because they were coming. And that I jammed all the clothes under the bed, kicked the shoes into a closet and made the bed with my pj's and socks still in it. And the irony is, they never believe that.

"Nawww . . . ," they say. "Your house always looks nice. I'm sure you make your bed every day."

Yes, yes, I do — every day that I know someone is coming over and will see it. Otherwise, I can't say I really care. Sometimes I make it, if I have three minutes. But typically the morning is much more about getting everyone dressed, fed and out the door. Not trying to prop and arrange nine designer pillows and a bolster.

So the doorbell rings and Leslie comes in. I show her to my room and she marvels that I made my bed. I tell her I only did it because she was coming, and she says she doesn't believe me because the room is so clean. And I tell her everything is hiding under the bed and the closet.

"Nawww . . ."

Okay, suit yourself. You wanna think I got up, made my bed, cleaned my room and scoured a tub before eight a.m., knock yourself out. Here's a fresh towel that isn't really that fresh. I wouldn't use that razor. And if you open that medicine cabinet everything behind the door will explode into your face. Enjoy your shower. I'll be at my desk.

Opening the mail.

It's a Wash

My washing machine broke down. Followed quickly by *me*. Because, take my vacuum, take my dishwasher, take my kidney, just please don't take my washing machine.

Wouldn't be so bad if I didn't have a huge load to do — the kind the kids are jumping into like it's a pile of leaves. And everything in there is some critical garment somebody has to have *right now* — baseball pants, a tae kwon do uniform, some dragon pajamas with wings and Mommy's only pair of loose-fitting jeans.

I try to decide if this is something I can impose on the neighbors. I mean, I've been there for them. They borrow cream, ladders and my *Vanity Fair*. Surely, I can do a spin cycle at their place, right?

Well . . . doing your laundry at somebody else's house is like having your hair done at the post office. It's awkward. Starting with the walk of shame up the sidewalk, carrying a giant basket of wadded up clothes. Talk about airing your dirty laundry. I don't know what's more disturbing to the neighbors — the fact that I have so many filthy clothes, or that I'm taking them out for a walk.

My neighbor quickly opens the door, hustles me inside and points me towards the laundry room. I think we both want to avoid the uncomfortable chitchat while I hold a basket of clothes between us like we're in some 1970s Tide commercial.

Slipping into her laundry room, I'm immediately confronted with what I'm sure is an exact replica of a space shuttle. What is this thing? And where are the launch codes? Because my Maytag top-loader is no match for this fancy Frigidaire stacked unit. And how am I supposed to get my clothes in the washer with the dryer sitting on top of it?

I call NASA and the laundry takes off. You can't actually fly this thing, but I bet you a hundred dollars you can heat a frozen pizza in it somehow. More weirdness ensues as I have to keep coming back to the house to check on my stuff. When you borrow a cup of sugar you're in and out. But when you're doing laundry you practically need your own key.

Fluff and fold isn't nearly as fun without CNN. In fact, I think the laundry room is the only room that I *don't* fold clothes in. Thankfully, my friend wanders in and we chat about fabric softener. Then I soak her nails in Palmolive and get out of there as fast as I can.

I've just got to keep our clothes clean. And the only way to do that is to wear the clothes we never wear. The kids don't like changing into their bathing suits when they get home from school, but suits are perfect to play in and I can hose them off before dinner. Only eight more days until the new washer arrives.

And I can stop wearing this tankini.

SWEET MOTHER OF ALL THAT IS HOLY

Everything looks good on skinny.
~ Somebody Who's Skinny

Yoga Pants Pose a Public Problem

Yoga pants are not *pants*. They're just not. Much like tie-dye has nothing to do with neckties, and gumshoes have nothing to do with shoes (or gum), yoga pants have nothing to do with pants, slacks or trousers and shouldn't be worn as such.

They're bottoms. Covering bottoms. For the purpose of being covered up during your high lunge, your half-moon, your revolved triangle and for heaven's sake, your down-ward-facing dog.

They are not for the purpose of running errands. Don't come bopping into the elementary school wearing bottoms when the dress code calls for pants that fit at the waist, and skirts that hit at the knee. You're wearing the equivalent of pantyhose. They're tight, they're shimmery, and the top's controlled. They don't have feet, but you line dry them, just the same.

If you can keep them out of the dryer, you can keep them

out of the school. And out of Starbucks. Which is where I learned this lesson, when I scooted in for a coffee after yoga and the guy behind me said, "I like it when girls wear yoga bottoms as pants. I wish they did it all the time."

Oh really? You do? Why is that? Is it because they make us move faster through the Starbucks line? I didn't think so, but thank you for making the distinction between bottoms and pants. And a case for a full-length coat.

So keep your bottoms out of Starbucks. And out of the grocery store. I hear people asking if you just came from yoga and you say no, you just threw on your yoga pants this morning because they're just so comfortable.

Which I don't get — how can you be comfortable? You're wearing spandex with a parka and your butt's hanging out. Aren't you cold? When you open the freezer to reach for that Lean Cuisine, don't you feel a chill? Slip on some sweats. They're warmer, and I promise you they keep the teenage boys from suddenly looking for Lean Cuisine pizza.

Try warm-up pants, because what you required for an intense side stretch is not needed to reach for the spaghetti sauce. If you need to stretch that intensely, I suggest you put on your heels.

But don't think that by putting on a pair of heels with your yoga pants, you're going to fool anyone into thinking they're leggings. Because yoga bottoms are skintight and shiny. This is the grocery store, not *A Chorus Line*.

Although I have to say . . . the last time I was shopping behind a gal who was rocking a pair of yoga pants, I didn't buy much. Not much at all. First time we ever had mineral water and kale for dinner. And I went to yoga every single day that week.

So, all right. You can wear your yoga bottoms to the grocery store.

Just call me so I can meet you there.

Botox? Or More Bangs for Your Buck?

Catching my reflection in a car window, I am shocked at my forehead. It looks like I slept facedown. On a rake. No wonder my youngest likes running his Hot Wheels across my face — it's practically a race track.

So now comes the question of what to do about it. I figure I have two options: bangs or Botox. Hmm . . .

Cost: Botox is definitely pricier. I hear they charge you by the vial, and the number of vials depends on your race track. And I can tell you that not even Jeff Gordon wants to go around this many times. But bangs are pretty cheap. You just go grab the kitchen scissors.

Pain: Botox is definitely going to hurt more. But then again, when you're cutting hair with something used to cut flank steak, you're probably going to get a few nicks.

Maintenance: Bangs will be a hassle. You have to keep them straight, styled and sprayed into place. With the Botox, you're pretty much styled and sprayed into place for the next three months, so nothing to maintain there.

Stare factor: Bangs on somebody are a major distraction for me. I find myself really studying them — their length, lie and texture. A girlfriend with bangs who finishes a thought with "so what do you think?" is going to hear something like, "I think your bangs are too short and they're not supposed to stick out from your head." Doesn't matter that she was asking what I thought about cooking a lasagna in a Crock-Pot.

Botox too, is a major distraction. The second somebody starts talking and I notice nothing's moving above the eyelashes, I'm consumed with solving the mystery of *has she or hasn't she?* Once I realize she can't blink, my thoughts turn to how many vials, how much money and how long before she'll be able to show emotion again. And then I wonder . . . if you can't emote, can you even *feel*?

Geography: Well, you have to go to a plastic surgeon somewhere to get the Botox. For the bangs, you just have to go to the kitchen.

Back to the cost thing: The bangs actually save money in two areas, because if they're long enough, not only do you not have to fix your forehead, but you don't have to do anything to your eyebrows, either. You wouldn't have to color, trim or pluck those things at all. You could have a full-blown unibrow under there and nobody would know. Just stay out of the wind. If they get blown to the side, it's going to look like you've got a ladder above your eyes.

I don't know.

Think I'll just wear a ball cap.

Here's the Skinny on Jeans

J. Crew's new denim collection is really annoying. It took me a long time to accept "skinny" as a pants style. But the J. Crew people have added Matchstick and Toothpick pants to the collection. What's next . . . Dental Floss?

They advertise the Toothpick cut as "Our skinniest style and the pair we're most likely to tear our closet apart looking for." I'm sure. Because you can't see them. In a closet full of regular-size clothes, it's the needle in the haystack. Hung sideways on a hanger, they completely disappear.

And when did marketing trade in fashion for fat grams? It's not milk. If you're going to label our clothes Skinny, Matchstick, Toothpick and Floss, you might as well use Whole, Reduced Fat, Low Fat and Skim. At least then I have options.

They also have the Boyfriend style — oh sorry, J. Crew calls it the Broken-In Boyfriend style. That must be the jean that the Low Fat girls tried to pull on and then stretched and ripped into their present shape. I guess at that point, you just cut them into shorts and call them the Napkin.

That's what I like about Loft. Their styles are named after women. The Zoe, Marisa and Julie. Zoe's waist and hips are the same size, Marisa's hips are proportionate to her waist and Julie has a small waist with curvy hips. Or is it Zoe who has the curvy hips and Marisa who has the same waist and hip size? Doesn't matter. It's not our business.

Nor is it our so-called broken-in boyfriend's business. Because if he's really broken in, he won't care if the label in our jeans says Matchstick or Marisa. But for the sake of argument, I think Marisa helps maintain the mystery.

Gap, however, is not interested in breaking it in, but rather breaking it down. Their styles are precise, with no wiggle room: Real Straight, Curvy, Sexy Boot, Always Skinny, Long & Lean, Perfect Boot, Curvy Boot, Curvy Skinny and Sexy Boyfriend.

I'll take Always Skinny and Sexy Boyfriend all day long. But I know life doesn't work like that. And trust me — Zoe, Marisa and Julie don't play that. If you've got them in your closet, Always Skinny doesn't stand a chance. Why do you think you people can't find Toothpick?

So imagine my delight when I walk into Loft and see the new Relaxed Skinny jean. Yes, by all means, let us please relax on all this skinny! I'm sure it's code for *standard* or *regular* or *human*. But it allows us to keep the narrow-minded title of Skinny, which any of us who've ever had a baby or eaten a Frito is just not.

And I can see them.

My Relaxed Skinny jeans — and the Fritos — I'll always be able to find.

It's Them, Not Us

Why do they call it *Us* magazine? They're not Us — they're
Them. I'm just trying to be like the PTA mothers — no way
can I go up against celebrity moms. We're not them and
they're not us, and I know this because I pump gas every
week without makeup on and it doesn't make the papers.

I know they want us to *feel* like the stars are just like us.
But I find that *they* do the total opposite of what *we* do . . .

They have a baby, then start dating, then get married.
And that's a cover story. In my family that's a scandal. And
then they give an interview about where they met — and it's
always on the set of some TV show. Or at their first ultra-
sound.

And then oddly they want the nursery photographed,
but not the children. Who wants to look at a baby album
full of twenty-six angles of a nursery? And instead of

monogramming the child's name on a nice blanket, they get it tattooed on their bicep.

And then they annul the marriage, citing fraud — which makes sense when one of them is an actor. And then they write a song about their ex, about how they're so over them and never think about them anymore. But then they sing it in thirty-two cities.

When they're not working, they're at yoga, and when they're not at yoga they're at lunch, and when they're not at lunch, they're getting something injected, and if they're not at any of the above, well, then they're in rehab.

They live in hotels, and they text whenever they need to say something to somebody. And they all think the presidential race is between Clinton and Sanders.

They go to Mexico when it's not even spring break. And they have more than one pair of sunglasses. And they always say that being a mom is their favorite role. Really? Because personally I'd love a crack at playing Roxie Hart in *Chicago* on Broadway, but maybe that's just me.

A typical night involves a ball gown and a red carpet and the typical wedding includes a castle and Wolfgang Puck, which makes the rare morning trip to Starbucks worthy of a full-page spread.

And they belong to unions and go on strike — during which time we see a few more Starbucks shots than usual. But they are offset by photos of what the stars do when they're not making any money, which is travel, buy new homes and shop.

Speaking of which, they wear the best clothes, by making the most money, doing the most fun job.

And they get awards. Acting awards, writing awards, directing awards. Best on-screen kissing awards, best on-screen fighting awards. And even if they're not the leading actor, or even the supporting actor, if they're in an ensemble of any kind with any of *them*, they get an award.

But they do give out that SAG award, so maybe that's their way of saying, *Stars — They're Flawed Like Us*. They don't ever say in their acceptance speech what exactly it is that's sagging — but they sure seem proud to have been nominated for it.

And the fact that they own it makes *us* feel a little better.

TROPHY MOM

When you come to a fork in the road, take it.
~ Yogi Berra

Pitch Imperfect

Watching a Yankees game on TV with my boys, I figured out what bothers me about baseball. Nothing ever happens.

There's a guy — pitching to another guy — hoping he'll hit it. Hoping to put the ball in play so the game can start. But there's no guarantee he'll hit it. There's no guarantee that *anybody* will hit it. In fact, it's such a possibility that no one will hit it that there's a term for it — it's called a no-hitter. It's the only sport that has a term for *nothing happened.*

They even created a position dedicated to catching the balls the batters don't hit. The catcher. He gets paid a million dollars to keep a four-hour game from turning into an eight-hour game by saving the batter from having to run after all the balls he misses.

But they're hopeful. They have another term for when somebody actually hits the ball, but still nothing happens: a perfect game — a game where they hit the ball, but nobody ever makes it to a base. To me the perfect game — at least the perfect game to *watch* — would be everybody hitting it and getting on bases and scoring runs. That sounds pretty perfect to me.

I feel bad for the batter because it's all on him. He's trying to get the game started while nine guys in the field watch. While his twenty-five teammates watch. While thirty guys in the dugout, forty-five thousand people in the stands and millions at home on their couch watch. No wonder he can't hit it.

A sport with the most people involved seems to have the least amount of action. Not much happens in golf, but at least they are in constant motion the entire four hours. In baseball, if somebody does hit the ball, the action lasts six seconds. And the guy's only gone ninety feet.

Best-case scenario, he does the biggest thing you can do in baseball, which is hit a home run. But even that only takes twenty seconds — and he ends up right back where he started. While Ernie Els ends up in the clubhouse with a beer in his hand.

Do you know how many pitches there are? Fastball, knuckleball, spitball, screwball — ten ways to throw it, but only one way to hit it. Seems to me they should throw it one way and come up with twenty ways to make contact with it.

But here we sit. Watching one guy throw a ball to another guy while somebody stands in the middle and takes swipes at it. If you think about it, it's really just a nice little game of catch between the pitcher and the catcher. And every now and then somebody interrupts them by hitting it. Baseball is interrupted catch.

I guess that's why every dad on the planet takes their son out to play catch. Because in the majors, if you're the pitcher or the catcher, then you're the one really playing baseball.

And everybody's watching.

Give That Mom a Medal

Climbing up into the chair to get a pedicure, the woman beside me is jumpy.

"I never do this," she confesses. "Someone gave me a gift certificate, so I thought why not? But I *never* do this."

Got it, lady. You're not here. I don't know who you are, or where you're supposed to be, but I didn't see you. No problem.

"I'm just really busy," she continues. "But I thought, okay, I'll take a little time for me."

Aha! Another mom with little kids. Trying to get out of the house and stay out of the psych ward. And so I go ahead and volunteer the chaos that is my life and tell her about my toddler getting out of his crib, curious if hers is doing the same.

"Well, I've got one in high school, one in college and one who just graduated."

Excuse me? You've got three kids who can dress, feed and drive themselves? And two of them don't even live with you? And you think you're busy?

She probably just woke up and this is her first stop. I got up at six. I made four breakfasts, dressed two people, packed three lunches and drove to two schools. Carved a pumpkin at one, hit a book fair at the other and then raced over here because my heels are cracking.

"I can't even remember that time when they were little," she offers.

Really? That's hard to believe, because it's burned onto my brain. I tell her what I can't remember is what my husband and I did all day before we had to change diapers and slice grapes. Not to mention a life before marriage.

"Yeah, my daughter got her first job and has an apartment — she loves it. She says it's just like college, but with money."

Terrific. Not only are your kids out of your house, they don't even ask you for money. This nail salon really shouldn't give out gift certificates. I ask what it is that she's soooo busy with . . .

"I coach high school volleyball. And swimming."

And then — very quietly — with a twinkle of pride in her eye, she continues . . .

"That one son I was telling you about, he's a swimmer. He went to the Olympics this summer, and Ricky won a gold medal."

Ricky? Ricky Berens? Ricky Berens who won the gold medal in the men's 4x200 freestyle relay setting a new world record, Ricky Berens?

She begins to tell me about their trip to Beijing. But all I can think about is that this woman birthed and raised an Olympian.

I can't even begin to guess how many hours she logged at the pool. How many hours in the car driving to practice and meets. How much money she spent, how much sleep she lost, how many sacrifices she made to help her son realize his dream. While raising two other children. And now she's coaching other people's kids to help them realize their dreams too? She's like, the busiest person I've ever met.

"You know, Ricky climbed out of his crib when he was a baby too."

And just like that, she remembers.

And suddenly, we're just two busy moms . . .

Talking about our babies.

Call It What It Is

Watching Bubba Watson swinging his pink driver at the Masters last Sunday, I was offered an Arnold Palmer . . .

A what? Oh, it's a drink? Mmm — bet it's good. I would bet the greatest player in the history of men's golf has the greatest drink in the history of bartending. Turns out it's just iced tea and lemonade.

This is succotash all over again. I remember thinking succotash was going to be some great dish, only to find out it's lima beans and corn. It's two ingredients. Why does something that's two ingredients need to be called something else — and who started this?

I blame the Cape Cod people. They took a simple drink — a vodka cranberry — and named it after a peninsula. Then they got nutty and added grapefruit juice and called it a Sea Breeze. Then they switched out the grapefruit juice for pineapple juice, and suddenly it's a Bay Breeze. And to really complicate it, they subbed orange juice for the pineapple juice, and ta-da: the Madras.

Instead of naming them after two breezes and a pair of ugly shorts, I would have named them after the two neighboring islands — the Nantucket and the Martha's Vineyard. Then named the third one the Ferry — because that's what you need to get to those places.

The point is the Cape Cod didn't need a signature name. It's two ingredients. Take a page from mac and cheese. Peanut butter and jelly. Pork chops and applesauce. They know how to keep it simple. Even the BLT had the right idea — call it what it is so we can all remember it. Because I promise you, nobody can remember what's in a Cape Cod. And even as I write this, I can't remember if what I was offered that day was a Jack Nicklaus or a Nick Faldo.

Now for three or more ingredients, you really do need a good name. A catchy, short name. S'mores is the perfect example. That's a short name for a lot of stuff and a lot of hassle. S'mores says graham crackers, chocolate bars, marshmallows, a fire pit, logs, matches, wire hangers, wet wipes and Neosporin for every kid who just can't believe a marshmallow really gets that hot. S'mores is perfect.

A good name and strong marketing will make it so that you never forget the name or the ingredients. Thanks to a 1974 advertising campaign, we can still to this day name all seven ingredients in a Big Mac. In under five seconds.

Oh well, whatever. At least now I know. So next year, when I'm offered a Bubba Watson I'll be prepared . . .

Iced tea — and *pink* lemonade.

They've Got My Number

There are two things I can always count on having in the front seat of my car — my garage door opener and my carpool number. So imagine my surprise when I pull up to the school and my giant laminated number is missing.

I panic as the carpool coordinator comes to the window, clipboard and radio in hand, her eyes squinting as she searches my windshield. And for some reason, I just keep starting new sentences.

"I can't find — I don't know where — It's always right — What in the — I can't imagine . . ."

I'm spinning. Where does a carpool number get off to? Did it fall out of the car? Is it stuck in the door? Did it slip under the mat or blow out the window or fall between the seats? Because there has to be a logical explanation for why something that only I use *every single day* would suddenly disappear.

It has to be the boys. This never happened before I had children. If I left something there, then it was *there*. But now my lipstick is in a box of crayons. And my ChapStick's with the glue sticks. My belts are part of an elaborate pulley system, and my sofa cushions make up three walls of a designer fort.

I don't get little boys. I don't understand why something that is mine becomes a version of something that is theirs.

The next morning I'm staring out the window at the mailbox, wondering if maybe the kids tried to mail it somewhere, when I hear this:

"Honey, you might have noticed your carpool number's not in your car."

Don't tell me . . .

"I left it at the T-ball field."

Come on . . .

"I thought of a great drill where the kids can throw at a target, and your carpool number is perfect because it's nice and big and square. And it has that cool clip on it, so I just clipped it onto the fence."

Immediately I flash to the T-ball field, where twenty moms watch the kids' dad clip #264 to the rusty chain link, laughing their heads off at the thought of me in the carpool line with all my doors open, swearing, "It's in here somewhere!"

I'm stunned. I mean, seriously? Is this really what little boys who use Mommy's hot curlers for bowling pins turn into? Grown men who use Mommy's carpool numbers for perfecting fastballs? I'd suggest hanging an old tire and using *that* for practice, but I'd probably come out to find my car up on blocks.

But now it's back. The crumpled mess that is my carpool number. Proof that any item of Mom's has a multitude of uses, of equal importance to many people. The laminate is peeled up on the sides. But counting the indentation marks left by the kids with decent aim gives me something to do at traffic lights.

So now I know.

Better go hide the garage door opener.

Covering All the Bases

Baseball is a hard game for kids. I think it's probably the hardest sport because there is so much to think about. But that doesn't stop us moms from telling our kids to just have fun. No matter what, there we are, telling our kids that having fun is all you need to worry about.

That, and not forgetting your glove. Or your ball cap. Or what position you play or where you are in the lineup or which side of the plate you bat from. But once you've got all that, just have fun.

So what if the bases are loaded and there are two outs and you're at bat — and you look over at Mom and she has her eyes closed because she just can't watch. And you're pretty sure you have to go to the bathroom, but know there's the play of a lifetime between you and the men's room. It's fun.

Just focus on that. And make sure your knees are bent, your elbow's up, your bat is back, your eye's on the ball and your mom has someone to cry on, that's all.

Then hit it. And drop the bat, don't throw the bat, and tag the base, don't miss the base, stay on the base, don't get off the base. And then holler to your mom she can open her eyes, it's over. And you didn't slide, so she doesn't have to do laundry. See? How much fun was that?

Now steal a base, GO! No, no, come back. Okay *now*! No, *back*! Uhh . . . *now*! No, no, forget it! Aww, inning's over. But that was fun.

And that's the whole point — just run on back to the bullpen. And find your bag and get your glove, and lose the helmet and find your cap — but that's not your cap, it's the pitcher's cap, go switch your caps, and find your base and hope the ball doesn't beat you there.

Now you're in the field — no pressure, just have fun with it. Look out for balks, bunts and pinch hitters. And glove ready. Down for grounders, up for pop flies and out anytime coach is looking. The play is at home base — unless it's at first. Though it might be at second, if it's not at third — but you've got eight-tenths of a second to figure it all out. And that's what makes it fun.

And when it's all over, doesn't matter if you won or lost. Just think about how much fun you had — and pack your bag, change your shoes, tape your blisters and get in the car and don't touch anything. And like Phil Mickelson recounting every stroke on the back nine of the Masters,

Daddy will recount seven innings' worth of plays, explaining where it worked and where it all went wrong — which is fun *and* informational.

Maybe this is why kids all over the world are playing baseball. Because moms all over the world are saying, "As long as you're having fun, nothing else matters."

I think we're a good team.

Let's Roll Up Our Sleeves

Planning my day at the Wells Fargo golf tournament with my kids, I click through the website and read over the list of prohibited items. And one item immediately catches my eye:

No Chair Bags (Folding chairs are permitted — the sleeve that holds them is not)

Thank you! Finally. Somebody who agrees that the "convenient" carrying bag is so unnecessary that it's actually prohibited at an event where the chair is permitted. The sleeve people had it coming. Give us the product, but for heaven's sake keep the aggravation of trying to shove it back into its synthetic shell.

I remember my first rain jacket that folded into a portable zippered pouch. Do you think I ever *once* got that thing perfectly pleated back into its puny pocket? Of course not. Because I didn't have time to take an origami class after each downpour.

Same with my sleeping bag. It always took my twin sisters folding it over and sitting on all the edges while I slowly rolled it up into a tight tube. And then one of us would hold the case while the other two blamed each other for not squeezing it tight enough, causing it to explode like a Slinky. This is where my dad came in; his answer to everything is bungee cords. And to this day, all our sleeping bags are bound in bungees.

But the beach tent tote people are the worst. Something you spent all day reading, eating and drinking underneath is not going willingly back into its sack. And not because the kids have been using the sack to collect shells in. But because nobody can figure out how to get the tent down. And once you use a power tool to dismantle a product, it becomes homeless. Unless you happen to save all those sleeping bag cases, which actually is not a bad idea for storing various pieces of tent, stakes and screws.

The umbrella sleeve people got it right. They instinctively knew that something with a metal spine that pops out and covers a human body isn't ever going back into something the size of a hospital straw. Their solution was to stitch on a strap with a snap.

Which really is all our chair needs. Spare us the embarrassment of trying to cram, jab and jam our chair back into its shell. Never remembering if it's seat or feet first, torquing and twisting it harder and harder, like we're operating some jackhammer, as we drill into the ground.

Plus, if you're having to fold your chair like a napkin and shove it into its holder after every hole, you're gonna miss a lot of golf. And if you carry your chair with one hand and the sleeve in the other, then you can't carry your beer.

Besides, sleeves may be prohibited. But bungees aren't.

Ace in the Hole

The kids are finally at an age that we can all play golf and tennis. And now that I've tried it, I do have a few thoughts on playing sports with kids.

For tennis, I advise ignoring the singles court. Just play anything inside the white lines. If the kids are under nine, just play anything inside the gate. And bag the service line, the service court and maybe even service altogether. Because to a kid, the precision required to hit the left service court with a tennis ball feels like trying to hit a fly with a dart.

Teach your kids the proper way to score, but then don't get cute with it. When it's 40–30, don't say "ad-in." When it's 30–15, don't say "30–5." And when it's 30–30 don't say "30–all." It confuses the children. And shows just how completely lazy we parents really are.

Also, don't bother switching from right service court to left service court. Or switching sides at all. Just put your kid in the shadiest part of the court and leave him there. Then you have something to punish him with. Poor sportsmanship buys you a spot on the hot side in the sun.

For golf, expect to see a lot of teeing up. Teeing on the box, in the fairway, in the rough and on the green. And don't be upset that you bought your kid a whole set of clubs, of which he uses only one. I think it's great when you can hit any shot with a 7 iron.

Props to my youngest, whose golf swing is the exact same swing he uses in baseball. And to my oldest, who twice hit the tee out from under the golf ball without ever touching the ball. True.

Oh, and driver's ed has nothing on golf cart driving. They learn to drive forward, backward, over bridges and over grass. And in circles in the parking lot, when you send them to look for the car. They even learn to appreciate infrastructure, once they're able to knock it in the fairway and actually use the cart path — as opposed to shanking it into the woods, turning our golf cart into an all-terrain vehicle.

But in both sports the kids seem to think flip-flops are appropriate attire, it being warm and all. Although not being able to run in flops actually keeps you from sweating. And it does make more sense when you're in a sand trap to be sporting sandals instead of spikes.

So maybe these kids are onto something.

MOM'S RECIPE FOR DISASTER

My mother's menu consisted of two choices:
Take it or leave it.
~ Buddy Hackett

Taj Ma Teeter Is Double Trouble

Whoa, Nelly, we got a new Harris Teeter. It sort of reminds me of Nordstrom. With cantaloupe. Like if you replaced all the shoes in the shoe department with produce, it'd look exactly the same. Except instead of the grand piano, Teeter's got a Willy Wonka glass elevator.

Because this place is a high fashion, high cotton, high-falutin "Oh, hiiii!" social scene. Which makes grocery shopping way more difficult.

From the moment you decide which set of double glass doors you're going to make your grand entrance through, you instinctively know that the days of buying Manwich and *Star* magazine are over.

My yoga teacher of all people comes towards me, and I swiftly scoot toward the sushi section and grab something that looks to be what we used for bait last summer, fishing off the Ocean Isle pier. She walks beside me, babbling about exercise while bagging pine nuts and cilantro in her reusable shopping bag.

I pass six neighbors, five school parents, a gal from book club and our youth pastor. How am I supposed to shop in here, with everyone taking little pokey peeks into my buggy?

So I follow little miss yoga pants and start shadowing her shopping. I get excited when she reaches for shredded cheese. But then she asks her kid to read the rest of the ingredients for baked tofu spinach wraps. Gross. Oh, and guess what's in an eggless egg salad. It ain't eggs, I can tell ya that.

But I've got another problem. All the shameful items are on the second floor of this ridiculous Taj Ma Teeter. The pharmacy, bathroom items, wine, chips and magazines are all up there together, and the only way down is the Wonka-vator.

Time to layer. In the bottom of my cart go all the pain aids, sleep aids, cabernets and chardonnays, Funyuns and Cool Ranch Doritos. Then I cover it all up with *Veranda*, *Good Housekeeping* and *Architectural Digest*.

I explain to my two little Oompa Loompas on the way down that we're going to have to eat some fish and veggies until we can get across the state line to a Piggly Wiggly. Because in the checkout line it's important that everyone admire your fresh salmon, beautiful squash and colorful radicchio.

And when the checkout girl reaches for my *Veranda*, close

to revealing my secret stash, I create a diversion — turning to the folks behind me announcing, "Hey, I've got this great recipe for tofu spinach wraps, would you all like it?"

Because nobody needs to know that I don't buy organic milk. Or that I need a Hamburger Helper. That I love the smell of Irish Spring, buy salad in a bag and drink SlimFast. I mean *geez* — if I wanted the whole world to know I use a plastic razor, I might as well write a book about it!

Oh — wait . . .

Getting Ribbed over Grilling

My girlfriend is caramelizing. Don't worry, it doesn't hurt. Although, it's killing me, because once again I'm left wondering why it is that I just don't try to learn how to grill.

It looks kind of fun. And easy. She's just standing there, flipping ribs, sipping wine. It really doesn't look that complicated. And she cheated anyway: she cooked the ribs in the oven first, and now she's rubbed something on them and is just turning them over and over again on the grill.

I think I can do that. Especially if grilling is baking, and caramelizing is drinking. It's in the bag. I start asking about her marinades, oven temp and cooking times. But the tall blonde in the rocking chair butts in.

"You don't need to worry about ribs. You just need to be working on hamburgers and chicken."

Oh, really? Who died and made you Barbecue Barbie? Just for that, I'm going start with kabobs.

Turns out a chicken kabob has more than two sides. I'd like to think that it's four, but I'm thinking it's more like four and a quarter. I've cut into it so many times to see if it's done, it's more like a chicken salad kabob. But I think it's cooked.

I could have closed the lid and cooked it faster, but isn't the whole point of grilling showing off for the neighbors? You have to stand out there and pose next to your grub.

Plus, you have to do it as slow as possible so you don't have to do anything else. You run the grill, you get to chill.

"Could someone set the table? I can't leave the grill. And can somebody bring me a plate and a fork? And water all these plants. And somebody get together a salad, slice some cucumber and tomato. And just reach into that cooler for me, will ya?"

I seem to be starting some sort of fire, and the smoke is really getting heavy. I wish my next-door neighbors hadn't opened the French doors that lead into their living room. Although, they have three kids and this would be a great opportunity for a pretty realistic fire drill.

"Could someone bring me some barbeque sauce, a knife and the garden hose? And just reach into that cooler for me, will ya?"

With the fire out and chunks of chicken everywhere, I decide to dismantle the kabob and go another way. I lay out all the veggies on the grill and start a little slice and dice. I'm

Kabuto. I cut off a small piece of onion and flick it off my spatula into the basketball goal.

And then put all the pieces of chicken into the bowl and mix in the sauce. Barbecue chicken salad with a side of grilled veggies.

I think I'm going to like caramelizing better.

A Race against Prep Time

Who exactly determines the "prep time" on recipes? I need to talk to them, because I slow-cooked a chicken parmesan with a prep time of twenty minutes, and they were *way* off.

It took twenty minutes just to find a pen and paper to make the grocery list. And then another seven to locate the Crock-Pot, find the lid, wash off the dust and answer my kid's question, "What is *that*?"

And because it was Veterans Day, the kids were home and wanted to go to the movies. So then I had to calculate just how quickly I had to slow-cook. Because for a noon movie, I'd have to fast-cook *after* the movie for four hours. But for a two p.m. movie, I'd have to slow-cook *before* the movie for seven.

Ten minutes to get to the grocery store, four minutes to find the baking aisle and nine minutes to locate black pepper, kosher salt and Italian seasoned bread crumbs. And a ladle,

I didn't have a ladle. Somebody used it to dig a hole and I haven't seen it since.

Fifteen minutes to collect salad fixin's, five to pick a loaf of fresh bread. But only four to put it all back in favor of a Caesar salad kit and a sleeve of garlic tear-n-share. Ten minutes to drive back home and bribe kids to unload the groceries with the promise of a movie sometime between four and seven hours. Three minutes to remember what I was making in the first place and another six to google it again, because the recipe on my laptop had been replaced with Minecraft.

Ten minutes to beat an egg, mix the seasoning and take a Tylenol. And then a whopping twenty-five minutes to roll the chicken breast in the breadcrumb mixture and have phone conversations with three moms about which PG movie we'll let our kids see.

Because it's impossible to answer an iPhone while you're breading chicken. The bread crumbs won't allow you to slide the phone to unlock. And even if you get it open, the crumbs stick to the face of the phone and you can't see the numbers to enter your password.

Nine minutes to find a can opener — not to open the marinara sauce, but to beat the jar with it so you can twist off the lid. But only thirty seconds to add cheese, because I cheated and bought shredded mozzarella, knowing I didn't have a grater. And shoving block cheese into a comb doesn't work — at least it didn't for us last time we made nachos.

So maybe the actual prep time for slow-cooker chicken parmesan is twenty minutes. But only if you have a full pantry, proper utensils, a photographic memory, no children and marinara sauce that pours from a fountain.

Or the phone number for Italian takeout.

Food for Much Thought

My brother-in-law is making cinnamon buns. Making them. And I don't mean banging a tube of Pillsbury rolls on the edge of the counter, hoping not to explode the container of icing in the bottom. He's physically rolling out the dough.

He says it's easy — just smear on butter, sugar and cinnamon, roll it up, cut it up and bake. But he always says that. He's just told me that the chicken salad I've pulled out of the fridge was easy too. So what's in it, anyway?

"Well, first I roasted a chicken."

Yeah right. If I'm roasting a chicken, the governor of the state better be coming to dinner. Because I'm not going to wait all day on a chicken to roast, only to cut it up into little pieces and make a sandwich out of it.

"Mayonnaise. And some mustard," he continues.

I'm always so impressed that Gary can remember every

single ingredient he puts into something. I can't remember what cereal I put in my milk this morning.

"Sliced almonds."

Here we go — this is where I decide I'm not even going to try it, because I'm sure I'll love it, but never be able to make it. So I just look at it. And try to identify each ingredient as he calls it out. It's sort of my own little I Spy game.

"Spring onions."

Found 'em.

"Thyme and rosemary. Sage and parsley."

Harder to pick out.

"Oh, and I sautéed the almonds in a little bit of butter first."

Oh, just stop it already, I'm never going to make this. At least not as long as there's Costco.

"Salt and pepper."

Notice how he never gives a measurement. Bet he doesn't even use a measuring cup, scale or spoon. He just eyeballs a pinch of this, a smidge of that — he's probably never even seen an actual recipe, just wings it.

"I added balsamic vinaigrette too."

Definitely not eating this. I'm not worthy. If you can't remember what you put in it, you shouldn't be allowed to eat it. And I'll never remember all this.

So now he's rolled up his cinnamon log and is cutting it

up into small buns. But suddenly, he stops — there's a problem. And I ask what's wrong.

"I — I forgot to put in the cinnamon."

Hmm. Maybe I *will* have some of that chicken salad.

No Hidden Agenda

You've probably heard about Jerry Seinfeld's wife and her cookbook *Deceptively Delicious* — about how to hide pureed vegetables in food. And then she was sued by another mom who wrote *The Sneaky Chef*. She claimed Jessica Seinfeld got the idea from her.

I just think it's hilarious that anybody would try to copyright what we moms are hiding. I mean, it's not just a recipe — it's a way of life.

For me it pretty much started right away. From the beginning, I hid the fact that I was even pregnant. From there I hid my age, my weight gain and six boxes of Thin Mint Girl Scout cookies behind the meat in the freezer.

During labor I hid my pain and the fact that I wanted another boy. And I hid the baby name book, with the name "Fletcher" highlighted with a big star.

I hid breast milk in formula, formula in cereal and cereal

in baby food. I hid peas in applesauce, fish in ketchup, green beans in hummus — and that was just my husband's dinner. I actually hid my fiber from myself, by sprinkling it on my salads and mixing it in my yogurt.

I hid water in the juice. Sugar-free cookies in the cookie jar. Any movie that had a *P* in front of the *G*. I hid the magnetic letters from *N* to *Z* because the whole alphabet cluttered my fridge. And I hid all the stuffed animals, cars and puzzles that talk, because it was just too much chatter.

Today, I hide breakables, valuables and toys that are obstacles. I hide Christmas presents, toy catalogs and any knowledge I have about Santa Claus, the Tooth Fairy and the Easter Bunny.

I hide my irritation watching my youngest take an hour to put a room back together that took six minutes to destroy. I hide my amusement when he asks me what *sarcasm* means, knowing one day he'll realize he's been drowning in it. And I hide any hint that I want him to be anything less than a big boy — when really all I see is a baby in a powder-blue jumper.

I hide that I turned forty-something and probably broke some record for oldest mom in the preschool. I hide my dark circles, my gray hair and sometimes the bank statement.

Before I know it the boys will be teenagers and I'll have to hide my car keys, my credit card and any sign that I just don't get kids today. And when they bring girlfriends over they'll make me hide their baby pictures, my *World's Greatest Mom* magnet collection and my fear that the girls might take them away from me.

But there is one thing I just can't hide. The new shipment of Thin Mints.

The freezer's full.

MAMA SAID THERE'LL BE DAYS LIKE THIS

Have no fear of perfection — you'll never reach it.

~ Salvador Dali

Getting Misty-Eyed

So I'm watching a preview for a new TV show called *Extreme Guide to Parenting*. And it shows a mom spraying her children in the face with some sort of mist from a bottle. The children wince and cough. And I cannot even begin to guess what she is spraying them with. Or why.

At first glance, I think it's sunscreen. But she wouldn't spray it all around their eyes. Same if it were bug spray. Plus, she's in her house. And while we are happy to spray chemicals all over our children, no way can we have it on our furniture.

Then I think maybe it's that Fairy Tales rosemary hair spray that is supposed to repel lice in your hair. But since she's spraying it in their faces, she would have to have really bad aim. Or the child would have to have really thick eyebrows.

It could be a hydrating mist. I used to use a facial spritzer to moisten my skin each morning. But people kept mistaking it for perspiration and thought I was terribly sweaty. I finally quit using it when someone stopped me on the street and politely asked if maybe I was having a heart attack.

Now, in the next scene, the clip shows the mom spraying it at her husband. And the thought crosses my mind that maybe it's some sort of magic potion to make him look more attractive to her.

And I really think I'm onto something when she sprays herself, because I figure she wants to reciprocate and make herself more attractive to him as well. But their faces stay the same. So either they're immune to it, or it's not a magic potion after all.

Maybe it's a stimulant that makes you want to clean your room, take out the trash and wash the car. With a tingling agent that makes you really excited about doing it.

Could it be something she concocted for school performance? Like a chemical mixture that makes you more focused and able to absorb larger volumes of material by moistening and opening your pores?

Or maybe it's an anti-bullying deterrent, something that smells really rank and keeps people from wanting to approach your child. Or maybe it's Perrier water and she's rationing it; I do that. I only let my kids take sips of mine — although spraying it seems like a waste.

Finally, I google the show. And it turns out it's an aromatherapy synergy spray — a fragrance used to alter a person's behavior or mood before they go out and do anything. Wow.

I would love that. If you could put yoga, sleep, Chanel No. 5 and a grande latte into a bottle and spray it at me, I'd be good to go.

But I'd still look sweaty.

Barking Up the Wrong Tree

I think about that tree riddle a lot: *If a tree falls in a forest and no one is around to hear it, does it make a sound?*

I want to do one. Mine would be: *If a Mom tells her children to do something and no one seems to hear it, did she say anything?*

Because I wonder. I can say it, holler it, scream it, and I swear nobody hears it.

"Put your shoes on, put your shoes on, put your shoes on, put your shoes on."

Nothing.

And ironically, it's always when I'm trying to get them ready for something that *they* want to do. Like trying to get them to put on their swimsuits so they can go to the pool. Or grab their gift so they can go to the birthday party. Or get in the car so I can drive them to the park. I'm a tree falling every minute. And yet, no one hears the thunderous crashing sound.

So back to the riddle — which asks if something can exist without it being perceived. And I realize that if my kids aren't hearing me, then I am not being perceived. And so basically, I do not exist.

Fine by me. I'm talking myself hoarse trying to get them ready for their next event, and for what? On the off chance I might run into another adult? And sit at the pool popping throat lozenges while we try to one-up each other on the number of times we have to yell at our kids to stop running?

How 'bout this one: *If a child has an event, but can't get himself ready to go, does the event exist?*

Nope. Not anymore.

So this is good. I don't have to say everything ten times. I don't have to say anything at all. I can just float around like some ghost. I don't have to tell them to come to the table to eat or get ready to go get ice cream or pick out a movie to rent or hang up wet towels for the pool party later. If they don't perceive me trying to get them ready for some real fun, then real fun will not be had. I'm happy to catch *Oprah*.

It takes a full day. But eventually they begin to perceive some realities. Like where did all these fallen trees and branches come from? And why didn't we eat today?

Poof. I am magically perceived. Even sought after. And they want to hear from me. With their ears peeled, they'd like to hear why it is that we haven't done anything, gone anywhere or seen anyone today. And why all the towels smell like the basement.

Talk about not seeing the forest for the trees.

But we'll save that one for another day.

Let's Do Lunch

I don't know why it's so hard to get together for lunch. I email my girlfriends a date, which we all have to weigh in on. Then a time. Then a place. And it's finally set. But then for all the days leading up to it, there is a barrage of texts asking when is it, where is it, what time and am I sure I have the date right?

How did we ever do playgroups? Back then, when the kids were babies, we successfully organized play dates. And not only were we able to find a day we could all do it, but we could schedule an exact hour and a half that fell after a feeding and before a nap, that we could all manage. Every week! We put our babies on our schedule, so that we could have time together.

And it's not like these things were easy. You had to be showered, dressed and packed. And by packed, I mean the diaper bag. You had to have drinks, snacks and a change of clothes — and that was just for you. Then you had to have bottles, milk, diapers, wipes, a changing pad and toys. All that, just to put all the babies down on a blanket and see who drools the fastest. But we did it, because we needed the companionship.

Same with the preschool. We'd sign up for the same stuff so we could all do it together. Pumpkin carvings, parades, parties and egg hunts were all done as a group. We craved each other's company and needed the adult banter. I've got pictures of us dressed in every costume imaginable — we were witches, elves, hula girls, even Jesus. And in that particular chapel skit, I played a disciple and actually washed my girlfriend's feet. Then we went out for Cobb salads.

But we made time, we got together, and I find myself missing it. With the kids getting older, so have we, and we are busier and more driven than ever.

We are going back to work, running PTAs, serving as team moms and room moms. We're taking care of sick parents, we're moving, exercising, starting new businesses and renovating houses. And there is no end to our kids' activities. We are just so busy.

But somehow for this particular lunch, we make it to the same place, on the same day, at (almost) the same time — and it's great. And we talk and agree to be more intentional about our time together. So when we're eighty, we'll still get together — and see who drools the fastest. We did it back then and we can do it now. We just need prioritizing, time management and commitment.

And calendars.

Mom's a Party Pooper

So my girlfriend asks if I'll go to a party with her. Great. What mom doesn't like being entertained and waited on in a house she didn't have to clean, eating food she didn't have to buy, drinking wine she didn't break the cork off of?

Walking into the party a few minutes fashionably late, my friend and I are still the first to arrive. And since I don't know the host, I walk straight up to him and introduce myself. And then he says, "I gotta take a shower."

This is a new one. I haven't been to a house party in a few years, but clearly things have changed. It used to be you get to a party, the host greets you at the door, offers you a drink, and then points out the chips and dips and pigs in a blanket.

Not this guy. He's going to bathe. But not before asking my friend to cut limes — and mentioning something about a DJ, a pot of chili, and warning that the western horse saddles draping all the barstools are not actually attached.

As the first guests arrive, I'm immediately asked where John is.

"Who's John? Oh, John! He's in the shower. We have plenty of fresh-cut limes. And chili, there's chili. No pigs in a blanket, but there's a DJ somewhere, hopefully not trying to ride a barstool."

This is why you don't leave hosting to your guests. Because we don't have any information. I don't know when John's coming down — or if we have any more limes, if the chili's meatless or why the bar area looks like the starting gate at the Kentucky Derby. I just don't know.

What I also don't know is why you post a nice invitation on Facebook telling friends that you're having a party with food and drinks, football and a DJ. But not mention what the party won't have, which is — well — *you*.

But just as I start to stir the chili, he descends the staircase. And I'm confused, because I don't know how to react. I've already seen him, so I'm not as excited as everybody else. Plus, I've been working — we needed more limes.

And I'm confused because I don't know how *he's* supposed to react. It's like he's walking into his surprise party — but he already knows we're there. Or like he's arriving at his wedding reception — but without a bride. He's making his grand entrance — in his own house. John has just arrived. From the *john*.

I don't know what to do. The only thing I can think of is to start a round of "For He's a Jolly Good Fellow," but it doesn't catch on. Everyone just seems so happy that he made it — downstairs. I'm happy too. With the host back in the saddle, I can take a break. Better yet, we decide to leave before it's time to serve dinner . . .

He's probably gonna need to shave.

Britney Cashes in Her Chips

The strangest thing about becoming a mother is that it happens in an instant. You literally go from being the child to being the parent in a single push. And it's not like you know what in the world to do — there's no manual for it — at least no one's mailed it to me yet. But I have this theory that our job is to plant a chip in their brain — that chip that discerns right from wrong, polite from impolite, moral from immoral, and *this idea is awesome* from *this is the stupidest thing I'll ever do.*

My theory developed back in 2007 when Britney Spears, in the middle of that epic meltdown, was getting her head shaved. And then she looked in the mirror and said, "My mom's gonna freak."

You got that right. But she isn't saying it because she thinks her mom is a nut. She's saying, *My mom will be disappointed.* She's saying, *This isn't what my mother wanted for me.*

This isn't how she raised me and this isn't what I'm supposed to be doing.

And that is exactly what I want my children to think when they are about to do something really stupid. I want to know that I have hammered respect and responsibility so far into their souls that they actually want to cry when they think about what they're doing and how it will affect me. Because that's the best gauge as to whether they should be doing it at all. It's like a built-in barometer. If it feels bad, then it probably is.

So how do we embed the chip? Well, it's painful. It takes a lot of discipline and a lot of consistency . . .

When they're toddlers it's all about reacting. When they try to open a drawer, you have to say, "No, NO!" When they throw something on the floor you have to *GASP!* And if they talk back you have to make your eyes really big so they think your head is going to explode.

If you do this consistently for the first six years, they hear "NO!" and *GASP!* and your head exploding before they even do anything wrong. It's like Pavlov's dog in reverse.

It gets trickier as they get older, because now you have to lead by example. And life gets really dull and uninteresting. Because you can't swear, overindulge, speed, gossip, talk on the phone while driving or take more than one free cookie at the Harris Teeter. One wrong move and you've basically given them permission to do it.

Sadly, they do it anyway. They break a rule or fail a test or leave their sweaty lacrosse socks in your car that smell so bad you're sure you're gonna have to sell it.

And then you have to go back to the reacting. You have to demonstrate all the disappointment and disapproval you can possibly muster — shame them so deeply they pray they never let you down again.

(Tip: Try not to show your pleasure at how good you are at this. This includes high-fiving Dad.)

It's tedious, but impactful. I really think if I embed all the data on the chip, they will instinctively consider the consequences and my reaction before they make a move. And I'm not talking about smelly socks now, I'm talking about drinking and driving, cheating and lying, and holding their moral compass upside down.

So son — my sweet son — see my face. Feel my wrath. Squirm under my burdensome disapproval . . .

And then let's check out the new Britney Spears album; I hear it's pretty good.

AFTERWORD

What My Mother Just Won't Do

I'm listening to the radio, and they're talking about what makes a great mom. And I start thinking about what I do that my kids would say makes me a good mother. Like maybe the four C's — cooking, cleaning, clothing and carpooling. But then I think about my own mother. And it's not what she does that makes her a great mom. It's what she *doesn't* do . . .

Starting with, she doesn't try to run my life. She has her own full, wonderful existence. She leads by example and hopes that I catch on. She never told me what classes to take, what sports to play or what friends to have. She found her passions and made great friends. It made me want to seek and find those things too.

She doesn't criticize me. Or my decisions. Like when I took a job at CNN in the late '80s that only paid $12,000 a year. And when I ran off to LA to work in the movie business, which is basically joining the circus, she didn't tell me to come home. Or to find a *real* job. Or to make sure I get to work with Tom Hanks.

She doesn't snoop, she doesn't pry, and she doesn't ask questions she doesn't really want the answers to. She doesn't play devil's advocate, and she doesn't judge. And when I go through rough patches, we log a thousand hours on the telephone because she never says, "I can't talk."

She never sugarcoated or covered for me or cleaned up my messes. But she never made me feel guilty. I was given the gift of true and complete unconditional love, whereby I could learn from my mistakes, suffer the consequences, but be forgiven and allowed to move forward without shame. She doesn't say, "I told you so."

She never asks, "Are you going to wear that, who cuts your hair and what's wrong with your eyebrows?" You'd be surprised how many mothers ask things like this. And she doesn't make me come home, or offer free advice or tell me how to raise my children. I get to make my own plans, my own decisions, and raise my children as I see fit.

So today, I'll try to remember that maybe it's not what I do that matters most to my boys. Maybe it's what I don't do.

By the way, I did get to work with Tom Hanks. And though she didn't say it, I could tell . . .

Mom was quite pleased.

THE END

Happy Mother's Day!

Acknowledgments

This Mother's Day I want to extend a big Mom hug to . . .

The Mom for All Seasons:

My Mother

Molly

For your patience, your wisdom, your wonderful sense of humor, your listening ear, your ability to find a place for any piece of furniture, your commitment to learn technology, your brilliance in coming up with the subtitle for this book, and your willingness to always be there for me through anything and everything. You're my prize. My true trophy mom. I love you!

My Sunshine:

Fiancé Andrew.

My Buds:

Sons Colton and Fletcher.

And future step-children: Allie, Jonny and Cate

My Warm Breeze:

Family: Jack, Molly, Kelly and Kristy.

The Spring Chickens:

Writing chicks Bess Kercher, Trish Rohr, and
Kimmery Martin.

The Cherry Blossoms:

Editor Betsy Thorpe, copy editor Maya Packard,
designer Diana Wade, cover designer Melissa
Gamez, web designer Christin Boone,
photographer Michael Newcomer,
and stylist Courtney Zepeda.

The Flowers:

All my readers who plant themselves in front of the
newspaper every week!

And the *Charlotte Observer* for giving me a place to
share my humor every Sunday.

CPSIA information can be obtained at www.ICGtesting.com
Printed in the USA
BVOW05*2018220316

441334BV00002B/2/P